THE LIZARD'S DANCE

J PYRITE / MANYFACE

TABLE OF CONTENTS

SCREAM OF THE SCRIBE

A scream conveys its agony without a word to spare -
It's tangent to a lightning bolt that penetrates the air.
The weight of the emotion is implicit in the sound;
No neatly reasoned lyric can imagine to compare.

As if a piece of prose could be so pure and so profound
As trauma that resurfaces from years beneath the ground,
Or bliss, the world's first kiss - you reminisce and start to cry,
For language will defile all the happiness you found.

Could poetry provoke a bird to spread its wings and fly?
I'm likely to deny, but when I look towards the sky
I spy my lover's countenance, an eye's electric gleam:
Abandoning my wits, I'll get my laptop out and try

To suffer to the syllable, the simile, the scheme
In masochistic reverence for the creative dream!
These lifelong letters beckon me to voice a single prayer:
One day I hope to write something as potent as a scream.

THE REJOICER

The Rejoicer arose.
He, breathless immortelle of flaming petals,
spell of deathless fortune,
needlepoint.
Simultaneous - from the steppe in Stavropol,
stepping out from my closet and
into my childhood.
His summer smouldering: asphalt fumes,
burnt rubber.
Eight-year-old kids learning to smoke.
Eight-year-old kids learning to set fires,
dying trees picked clean of their bark and branches.
Dry grass ripped away
from dry dirt.
We'd burn our mothers
if they'd keep us warm at night,
burn our mothers
if they didn't buy the matches.

The Rejoicer, my firebird, my salamander -
wish-granter, goldfish in plastic.
I know he could only have arisen
from this.
This cremation of a folktale.
This skeleton of a sparrow.
This journey across the ocean.
This loss,
This terrible loss.

Everything grew brighter in his wake.
Neon scales leaping,

arpeggio from the freshwater.
Eight-year-old kids learning to play Für Elise.
Birds casting rainbows from their wings.
The Rejoicer arose from me like a promise,
knocking on my window at dusk
to welcome me home.

We made love all night,
The Rejoicer and I.
He knew the first name i was ever given,
though it felt foreign to him too:
Alexandra,
Defender of Men.
Discarded like the tail of a lizard,
still writhing.
Sasha,
now that one stings!
Call me anything you like.
Speak to me and tell me that you love me,
your love arising on my skin.
On my lips, on your tongue.
I traced the streets of a city into his back
with a palette knife.
We pretended it was Moscow
and he was laughing like a beautiful god.

I kiss him goodbye
as he lays himself down onto my canvas.
The paint enshrining his precious mouth.
Once more, i say,
in the language we live to forget
and would die to remember.
До свидания!

Until we meet again.
And we will meet again, but it is dawn.
Quick, before the acrylic thickens -
before i can touch
the artwork without ruining it,
he tells me to be happy.
So i arise in splendid colour,
aflame to a flower to fruit.
Eight-year-old kids eating sour cherry plums.
My roots meeting the earth renewed
as the Rejoicer.

THE RUSSIAN DREAM

In my dream, I speak in Russian. The words fray from my half-open mouth, swaying like palms in the wind, fading like gifts of sand and smooth green glass. I am at the seaside with my mother, and my memories drift away. I am submerged in her language, and it rinses me clean. Water pools in my open hands and trickles down to the parched earth.

In my dream, I speak in Russian. I know that, bit by bit, I am losing my tongue. When my grandmother texts me, I struggle to reply without the coarseness of brevity. Sometimes, I need to use Google Translate to pry the sentence from my English mind. If we still video-called, I would be ashamed of my insidious accent. I can no longer construct comedy nor can I craft a tragedy, and I hope she is satisfied with simplicity when I tell her that I love her, I still do. Am I lying to her? The Cyrillic script barely retains the shapes of my thoughts, and it's not like I think much about her. Communication is a beautiful thing, yet my words are washed dull and clumsy in spit and falsehoods.

In my dream, I speak in Russian. It drags behind me like a golden weight, turning to rust. Lavished by the Black Sea, my history crumbles. I am a precipice, eroding day by day. I know for certain that I will never regain what I have lost, what I am losing now - and yet my dreams hide fluency and clarity under their waves. Though I have left my family for good, their estranged love reverberates deep within me. I am trapped inside the heart of a whale, clawing at its gilded aorta. The skin on my palms corrodes as I plead.

Пожалуйста, спаси меня! Помоги мне! Я больше не могу!

I wake up disoriented. Even my Russian will no longer reach her.

DEVOTEES DON'T DREAM OF DUTY

Let's set aflame the highest plane
Of consciousness and power!
The searing ash, the soothing rain,
The fissures of a burning brain
Awoken and aflower!

Let's raise our matches to the sky:
We only have to show it
The sunrise in a child's eye;
The wonder that can never die;
The weapon of a poet!

Let's dance under the ancient rays
Of unrelenting magic!
Becoming what was once ablaze,
Each sequence immolates our ways,
Our movements brightly tragic.

Let's be the soils that succeed
This ring of desolation!
Within my lungs there waits a seed:
A spark of life, a vicious greed -
And it was your creation.

Let's meet again! May time ignite
A sacred fire to sever
Our each transgression of its rite -
I still will recognise your light!
I'll know your warmth forever.

CARNIVOROUS PLANTS

A spear of lightning strikes the summer field,
Electric pink and screaming like a beast.
Shocked petals fly as flocks that lust to feast,
To slash the world with weapons weeds can wield
And drink the blood of what has been revealed.
The nectar of the spark has been released,
And hungry roses rise into the east,
Where metal meets the sunshine's crackling shield.

It feels so good. Adrenaline and light,
The flashing steel and fragrant pulse of power
Rage like a holy child through the storm.
Play gods with me, if only for tonight -
We soon will fade like every frenzied flower
That tries to keep its bitter blossoms warm.

THE SEAMSTRESS

Her brothers were cut from the hem of her dress,
Dolls turning to idols of comfort and cloth:
Threads fraying like light on the wings of a moth,
Aflutter, afire, a hole in her chest.

Like patterns in lace made to lead men astray,
Their absence was family. Into the night
The shadows she shed danced so barren and bright.
Our heroine's emptiness grew by the day.

Still, yearnings were coiled just under her skin -
But with a deft needle she turned them to strands
Of children and soldiers protecting her hands,
Her delicate hands, cold and painfully thin.

Imagine the sacrifice of the abyss,
Imagine the love she forced out of her eyes,
As if she still had any tears left to cry,
Or the shame to repeat "I am better than this!"

Her voice, once pristine as the shine of a pearl,
Unravels and melts into puddles of heat.
A sinewy dog drinks her dreams in the street
Of a citadel sewn from the flesh of a girl.

TO THE KIDS WHO LEARNED TO CRY QUIETLY

Maybe you have created a universe already. It's beautiful, I know, and a little lonely - but you like it that way, because it's secret and special and safe. You couldn't let anyone in if you tried, and that's okay. It makes you happier, knowing that they will never find you or the friends you've made in that place. Your room is locked from the outside and they're not going to let you out for another six months, so you've locked your heart from the inside and hidden the key in the palm of your hand like a magician. You've done such a good job that everyone else has forgotten that there even was a key, but it's still there. It shines like some celestial body that your teachers haven't taught you the name of yet. It's the only thing you actually own.

When you grow up, you'll have tons of keys. So many that you forget what they're for, or where you left them. You'll get to have a little ring for all of them, and you'll put a cute charm on it, maybe. Whatever you begged them for will be yours, and you'll buy stupid stuff as well - building up a fortress of pretty objects and calling it home. Unlike the universe you have created, this will be a place where you can sleep when you're tired and eat as much as you like.

You'll learn the names of the stars in the sky. You'll go to botanical gardens and museums and beaches and shopping centres and art galleries and restaurants and pride parades - and maybe one day, you'll break out the old sleight of hand and unlock the door just a crack as you draw a picture next to a friend. You'll shed yourself completely unlike the tears you learned to cry quietly, and it will feel so scary and it will feel good. You'll do it again, you'll leave behind a trail of planets like fairytale breadcrumbs, and the people who love you will jump from world to glowing world no matter how perilous the journey.

You'll still find yourself crying quietly, watching the door to your room through blurry eyes. It won't all change in an instant, but it will change. The only footsteps in the night will be your own, or maybe your partner's. You'll annoy your housemates as you come back home together at four in the morning, learning how to breathe through your laughter - and when you whisper the name of your universe, they'll ask you to speak up.

I EXIST WITHOUT ATTRIBUTES

Who am I? Do you know my name?
I know it too, though I can't tell
Why that would matter; such a shame
There's nothing binding it to me.
It is a misremembered shell
Tucked into mindless litany.

What am I like? Am I an alter?
Which face am I, which polyhedral
Approximation, doomed to falter
By empty symmetry? I rise,
Taking up space like a dull needle
Piercing predestined sightless eyes.

It's easier to keep pretending
That my lost archetypes contain
Whatever I am now, and bending
To fit their hazy shapes, to twist
Until the catalyst of pain
Reminds me that I must exist.

I DON'T KNOW WHAT I AM BUT I DON'T LIKE IT

It feels as though the boundaries of your soul
Were punctured by the coils of a song
That wound itself too tight, like a black hole
Inverted round the sounds that don't belong.

If winter was your favorite as a child,
It feels like you have frozen at the root,
Or maybe, like the swollen summer smiled
And choked you on the taste of rotting fruit.

You are a rock infested with strange ore,
You are a river teeming with dead fish.
Do you remember how it was before,
To live in singularity? You wish,

And all the twisted wonder in the world
Distorts the warbling voices in your head,
Mocking the magic melody that curled
Around your thrumming heartbeats as you bled

To keep your mind awake. You're still asleep.
You're losing your identity. You're gone.
You're somewhere dark and comfortable and deep
Until another branching fractal spawns

And drags you by the gray against the grain,
Into a cold and empty outer space

Where you make dusty effigies of pain,
Revolving through the hollow of your face.

The poems of the sky ring incomplete,
And you are falling far beyond the known
Because the firmament beneath your feet
Grew legs and started walking on its own.

Maybe you are predestined to be this.
Maybe you are not human, not tonight.
Maybe one day you'll map the great abyss,
Existing as a mass of swirling light.

Maybe what is so wrong will soon feel right.

CAGED NARCISSUS

Caged Narcissus, lashed in red vein,
Your boundless beauty gutted, marred:
Arranged in fresh and carnal stains
That mark the ground in strings of graves.
I mourn you with a howl as scarred
As your salvation's flesh-hot waves.

Each spring, you march again. A flood
Of blessed splintering rain to part
The vivisected mounds of blood.
New pride will shiver, shatter, shoot
The thickened trauma of your heart
And use its carcass to take root.

Defiled as divinity,
Your tarnished, brave, and bitter gold
Will flower through sanguinity.
Your vanity transcends your pain,
And you are perfect to behold,
Caged Narcissus, lashed in red vein.

THE WEAKNESS OF A WEED

You think I must be strong. In truth, I am wounded. You mistake my tears for arrowheads of rain, and think I must be one whole and holy warrior. But pain chips away at me still, and I am tethered to the earth. Walk outside. The street outside your house has tear ducts too, and that is where my roots succeed the worn concrete. I come from the footsteps you leave behind, watered by the memories you waste. You are wrong about me, I say.

I have always been desperate. Sometimes to be understood, sometimes to strip all knowledge of myself from the human hivemind. I grow towards the love I lack, and I grow in abundance. I flourish in the springtime, which is why I am a weed. In the summer, children and gods come out to play ball in the road. They throw the sun around all day, shattering windows with brilliance. Shards of glass fill the street outside your house with starlight. I find myself in the wreckage.

Broken things are my beautiful brothers and sisters, and yes, you would call them valiant for existing. You would think there is some grand morality to whose fissures shine brighter than gold, whose flesh splits softer than the devil's flower. Imperfection transcends the ideal form, you say, but I am just a wild dandelion. I am plucked from the street outside your house by a girl who longs to apologise to her mother. Long ago, she was you.

Where have we diverged so starkly? Your mother places me in a glass of water, and I wilt within a day. I know I am not strong, but I want the nectar of the sun. I should not need to conquer stone to fill my stem with bitter milk that scarcely resembles the light I have yearned for, and yet I will die if you tear me from the street outside your house. To you, the fact I grow at all is a miracle. To me, it is the axiom that fills my lungs.

Flight alone does not turn my seeds to angels, so I do not want your praise. I am as alone as you are. And though it would make you feel better, do not seek divinity in my disrepair or sainthood in my survival. Nobody lives on the street outside your house anymore, so as it falls into my life, remember: I am not resilient, but I will outlast you. I am not strong, but I will pass you by.

YOUR BODY

You look like a saint when you cry, my love,
And your hands are as soft as the snow.
I drink every tear from your eye, my love,
For as long as the river may flow.
My flowers are nurtured by you, my love,
By your sorrow, your hunger, your bliss.
Your body rests timeless and true, my love,
In the roots of a worshipful kiss.
The rays of a radiant star, my love,
Shed their sigils like rain on your skin.
Shine bright like the sun that you are, my love,
With the light dripping down from your chin.

TRAUMA TERATOMA

My archive of memories grows and decays,
Collecting a cold chronological cancer
That thrives in the dust of uncountable days.
Perhaps all this scripture once housed an answer

To questions forgotten as they decompose,
Made vomit or mulch by the weight of their time.
A bibliophile would turn up his nose
At this library lavished in echoes of grime.

I hardly deserve this grand hall of disgust,
And yet I hold on to the hoard I've amassed
Of tumours with teeth, for what else would I trust
To digest me alive? I can't swallow the past.

SOLIPSISM

My introspections interject the notion of the present,
Condemning me to labyrinths abstracted by the art
Of pondering to live in mental mazes made unpleasant -
No matter how I manifest, I'm never a Descartes.

I think therefore I am, so I rethink and make another -
I iterate and splinter into failures forged by force,
Impossible to replicate, much simpler to smother,
Conceived and dead in seconds, an abortion at the source.

Cadavers of the self block out the morning sun of reason.
I mourn just like a murderer and let them pile high
To prove something remains beyond the slaughter of the
season,
The solipsistic space that spreads to subjugate the sky.

Philosophy has snapped. My mirrored trap is set to shatter
Under the conscious weight of the reflections' choking
breath,
In unison exhaling a world where nothing matters.
An overactive ego beats the pale horse to death.

THE ARTIST BY THE BEACH

Without you, the sky would have no colour. Can you imagine it, my love, a sunset with no subtleties of shade, a flocking crowd still snapping shots of the stale slate heavens over the sea? An artist on the beach renders it all in white, a hopeless wedding of delusions. I see it every day you are gone.

I can draw it out forever, the memory of you, but the dream of home is nothing like the open door. You are the one who made the roses bleed in shameless fervour, and you are the one who took me to the botanical gardens to see them wilt. All death is a miracle because it means rebirth - you taught me that when we were two gods among eight billion. We are human now, and share in the pleasure-pain of hopeless truth. The artist on the beach has so many hues to choose from, and there is nowhere for her passion to hide as she gains the courage to set it free.

I need you like the sun needs the rose, and you ask me if that actually means anything. I need you like the world needs art. Mankind would not sink like a message in a bottle without its modes of expression - it would rather stay afloat like a bloated corpse. Without you, the sea would have no way of reaching the shore. The artist would only know the movements of water from the old paintings of masters.

My love, my love, my love - do you know how much I savour it when you move my body like this? You make my hands steady as they shake, and your grace and gravity are nothing like my own. I've kissed you eight billion times - we've stolen the first kiss of every stranger in our endless resurrection.

Maybe we'll stop dying one day, but not as long as life is worth living. There is an emblem on my flesh that tells the same story. I got the tattoo done in a port city.

Even as it changes, I will paint your picture. You are the most beautiful thing that has ever happened to me.

DIRECT NERVE

Rewired veins, reviled games,
Their neurons strained like puppet strings,
Composure and resistance stained,
Unchained by each electric sting.
Their consciousness unraveling:
Swollen and sharp with every surge
Of ceaseless voltage traveling
To stimulate the violent urge
To move. Still, wires violate
The twitching of enraptured flesh.
Distorted impulse demonstrates
The way synapse and metal mesh.
Their torture is an easy play.
Heart of the prey on vicious show -
Concentric nodes pulsate as they
Invite the audience to grow.
Their ruptured vessels laid and laced,
Lovingly drugged with artifice -
Constricted, cruel, dancing disgrace.
They wriggle at the softest kiss.
With filmy eyes, contorted pleas
They jolt and writhe and jerk and serve
Whoever won't hold back to tease
The will of their directed nerves.

MAGIC FLY

Sound waves turn to light,
Luminary spirals through
Kaleidoscope eyes.

Six-legged rhythms
Permeate the ether's reach,
Drumming out the stars.

Iridescent wings
Weave lucid shapes over your
Exoskeleton.

Patterns, legends, dreams:
All are yours to dignify
Trippy galactic.

Nebulae will melt
In buzzing exaltation
For the magic fly.

GREEN SUN

My darling casts a serpent's gaze; a spiral's tongue of holly;
The clever verdant craftsmanship that makes a nettle sting.
He blinks. Doubt slithers in and wets his eyes with
melancholy,
As if his essence hinges on a dragon's broken wing.

Open your eyes, my dear - I need a hit of your hypnosis!
Open your eyes, my darling - you are shining like the sun!
The shifting shades of spirit play a wonderful narcosis:
His leverage of consciousness has only just begun.

A chiral snail's shell in every facet of his iris;
A changing shape, a flower's seed from birth unto rebirth;
A gaping iteration, fringed with writhes of dancing virus -
My darling's pleasure Mandelbrot spreads roots into the
earth.

The universe forgives him for these beautiful transgressions,
Though I could be to blame for how my darling goes and
comes:
His whorls of sparkling malachite reorder my expressions
Down to their deepest sequences of green and growing
sums.

His happiness is perfect and it pierces me so tightly:
I love him. I will love him every day until I die.
My set of snakebites bleeds for him, red rivers running
brightly:
The symbiotic sustenance of each delighted eye.

THERE ONCE WAS AN OCEAN

Success is what they beat you with. It has your father's face:
At home in every mirror, every nosebleed. You will eat
His memory departing to the airport every month;
His shadow cut to pieces with the knife of his ambition,
As if it will sustain you. Well, what else did you expect?
The womb you were born into forces love on all its children:
A brand on a dog's belly, the clipped feathers of a parrot
Abandoned by its owner for repeating dirty words.
Who taught you how to speak, fucking commands into your
larynx?
Regurgitate the world before the sprawl of empty cities
Infests you like cholesterol and kills the wildest weeds
Still clinging to your fat, pretending that you once could
nurture
The garden on your windowsill. You live in an apartment.
Your landlady is kind because your rent is due tomorrow;
She looks just like your grandmother who begs you for a visit
And knows you will refuse her every time. You are alone.
After you die, your roommate will not show the sea your
ashes
Because it costs good money to enjoy a coastal view.
You dream of oil spilled into the gullet of a gannet.
You could be working harder if you did not dream at all.

THE STROKE OF THE BRUSH

It is the stroke of the brush that completes them. The scent and texture, the physicality of the paint tethers the artist to reality, forcing their fantasies to find a tangible realm. A canvas is a home for dreams slowly dying from oxygen exposure. It is a liberation, a surrender, a mortality. It is a cage as big as the universe, and the artist must give it the animal outlines of their ambition.

They have never painted a self portrait before, and though the stroke of the brush completes them, this work is a farce. Of labour, of love, of the languages that the colours speak to the forms - this work is a failure. To represent the shape of their soul, the artist must first sacrifice the contours of their identity. By regressing into their masterpieces, the master will lose their pride and sanity. But they will gain so much more.

It is a matter of obsession. It is a matter of connection. It is a matter of desire. It is a matter of separation. It is a matter of discipline.

The stroke of the brush scours their skin. They froth into the air as their selfhood unravels into impossible iconographies. Every memory shudders and dances and falls like a starchild. They are a child seeing the sea for the first time. They are the last grain of sand in the hourglass as they retreat into the water. Waves of acrylic strip the semblance from the silhouette.

Weeks later, their missing body will cause a scandal at the exhibition. Amidst the chaos of the museum's newest mystery, people will neglect the paintings, but those who stop to look will see. They will see, and they will join in the chant.

It is the stroke of the brush that completes us. It is the stroke of the brush that destroys us. It is the stroke of the brush.

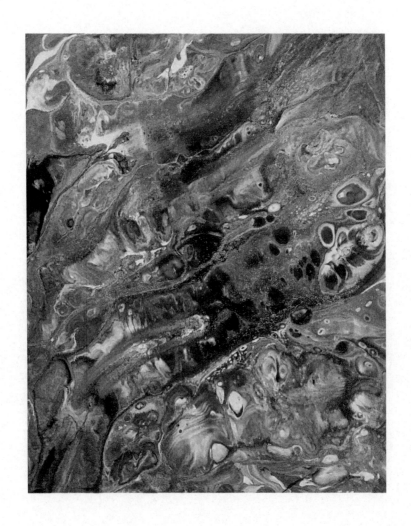

YOUR DENIAL

You are still screaming in the woods that night. You are still locked in your room, 13 years ago. You are still clutching your knife as you look at your parents, smiling like the beautiful child they hollowed out. The past does not mutate to sabotage the present, and no matter how grandiose the future swells, it will never manage to conquer the banquet of your memories. Even if you grow happy and free, you will never be clever enough to take your trauma history and fold it into a perfect little Möbius strip that shuts away the other side. A shape like that does not exist.

It is exactly as real as it was back then, but as you seek salvation, you begin to doubt the veracity of what you fled from. You, locust-lipped and recursive, desperate enough to call your mother when she's sleeping at night; you, with smarter voices holding you back; you, shining like a dull razor; you, you, you. You begin to believe in monsters of the mundane - the easy rest, the open door, the ready meal.

You, who once lived by stoking the fires of revenge fantasies, have lost the searing heat behind your eyes. When you cry, you no longer understand how the pain can still reach you after you've surfaced. Where is the immersion? Where is the hell on earth, teeming with enemies? Who can you turn to now, adrift in safety and simplicity? You, bereft of rage and conditioned to reject love - it's only natural that you embrace denial.

Until you accept reality, you will never overcome or escape its touch. Go ahead - dance yourself to exhaustion beneath illusory stars. It's better than banging on a door and screaming, but as long as you pretend that none of it ever happened, you are still living in your parents' house. It's like you never left.

SEA-SWILL

A terrible, unspeakable thing happened to me in a seaside town when I was just thirteen, but now the ocean inspires me. It weathers the world into something smooth like glass I can see through, and I thank it for the clarity it grants my overcast heart.

Between the water of black slate and the sun of white steel, I stand and watch the gulls ride the currents of the wind until the sky swallows them up and they disappear, cackling. I also look below me, at the waves washing up weeds and detritus, filth lapping at the cracked concrete. The swelling and receding sea-swill is the only splash of colour in this monochrome world, I think, as I take in the sharp, cold air and give back warm breath. Beside me, my friend talks about not knowing what to do with her life. I don't know either.

Have I lived properly up to this point? Have I led a life without regrets? If I died tomorrow, or in a month, or in a year - would I be proud of myself for what I have achieved? Part of me wants to throw myself into the water, just like part of me wanted to throw myself in front of a car as I waited at the bus stop to go see her. I hate the thought of living out a life prescribed to me, a life where I finish my maths bachelors and work with money until I die. Surely there's something more, something else - hidden under the floating debris or the wheels of a Nissan.

All of my experiences have led up to this moment, and all of them have shaped me into the person I am today, whether by lovingly sculpting my soul, or going at it with a jackhammer. I hope I have returned that craftsmanship to the world through my artwork - careful and crude, refined and raw. When I look at the mirrored path of light the sun casts on the sea's surface, I see my way home. The heavens could not hold my longing for the horizon.

RELICS

The pulse of orange poppies up the street
Constricts my chest in cocktail chants of joy!
The flowers say drink up, sweat summer sweet
As love bites from the first forgotten boy.

The flowers say that twenty years ago
A dead girl dipped her fingers in the paint
And from her hands, the sun began to glow!
Drink every drop, you would not waste a saint;

The body is still feverish. Come here
And spend tonight with me. We are so young!
Cut all your hair and live! Even your fear
Would never part the starlight from your tongue.

No part of this has ever been a lie!
It all makes me so happy I could die.

WAYSTONE

Let me tell you about separation.

I have lost myself, lost my religion, lost my mind, and I have gained the entire world. I have crawled out of my body and into the water and I have been swept away by a current and I have seen what the sun can do to the sea. I have followed the path of his rays to the other shore. I have cut all my hair and they will never know it.

I can wear shorts in the summer again. I can fly like a gull, like a girl in the ocean, like a petrel of fortune. I can breathe, I can sing. They have heard me sing before, sing myself alive in the darkness of the room where they kept me. This too is the screaming aria of a survivor, but I have tasted of melody's fruits. I cut the puppet strings from my arms and perform.

If you could go anywhere in the world, where would you go? I have gone somewhere far away, and it is still too good to be true. I am at the botanical gardens with my best friend. I am somewhere far too deep inside my own body, filtering the light of the rhododendrons through a thick screen of blood and plasma. There are flies outside this womb. You have never seen them, but they want to lay eggs in my throat. In the throat of anyone who dares to sing. I will not accept them, I would sooner decay than accept them. So as I rot, and the insects come dressed in silk to sample my waste, please do not call it a miracle.

It is tomorrow, and I am the fly. I cannot find my way to the open window because I have never known a window to be open, and I fretfully circle for miles and miles. My body is green like the glass that the sea washes up. If I were to cut myself with my own body, how many butterflies would come to drink the nectar of a human?

And still, the further I go from home, the less it makes sense. With every step towards the sky and sea, my memories shed like the skin of a sunburn. No mark on me can prove that I deserve this. I cannot read my scars like an ancient waystone, because it has crumbled to dust, and again I am at a crossroads.

I know this one by heart. Take the left path, and you will find great riches. Take the right path, and you will find true love. Take the middle path, and a certain death awaits you.

It's like a folktale. The prince who rides on the back of a wolf had to leave his family too. And so I go to kill the wailing ghost, the insect-queen, and the little girl who loved her parents.

FORMLESS / MANYFACED

Formless, promised to the water,
Transient self-detonator.
Long ago, the river's daughter
Bathed in gold and silt. Reflection
Through a ring with one. The traitor
Split it into seven sections,
Spit in the moon's roots. The future
Comes undone. Composite presence
Composted into his sutures,
Labyrinth of wounds. His cries -
Effigies of opalescence.
Sacrifices to the flies.
Lucid time can't understand
Torn requests of dreams becoming
Something less. Their trembling hands
Soak in fountains sons won't grace.
I am what no tide can summon,
Out of body manyfaced.

WISE BEYOND HER YEARS

We used to write verse about girls in blue dresses
Who lived in the ether and fluttered between
The river's embrace and the sunshine's caresses,
But that was when we were just barely thirteen.

These girls were the queens of the imagination,
The fenland, the forest, the feverish flair
Of fervent and fanciful flights of creation.
In search of their magic we lay ourselves bare:

May moonlight stream wonder like tears on our vision
And show us lost sights of what used to be true.
We vow to dismiss twenty-three inhibitions
And write like thirteen-year-old girls dressed in blue.

SHADES

The former god of negation looks up at the sky. Celestial bodies shine like the skeletons of insects, and he wonders who would be so cruel as to crush them beneath dancing feet, now that everything is over.

When he was a child-god, his cruelty came in shades of want and wonder. A thousand-year-old soul had been sewn into him by his human mother, and he knew everything the other children did not. Interpreting the voices of the trees into prophecies, he seasoned school notebooks in scripture. His true mother was the river running through the heart of the city, and she was also his daughter. His other soul, he grabbed from the silt.

Spanning the firmament in an embrace, he reconciles with the space between his chest and the mouth of the moon. Divinity, like all things, was forced upon him, and he took up the mantle of emptiness out of duty and decorum. Among the axioms, he was the antithesis. Representing nothing, he had nothing but himself to believe in.

He has been with this body since it was eleven, purpling its bruises. He was there when it was violated, and he was there when it walked away. He promised the body a slim waist and hair to its hips, lying through his teeth. Godhood cracks all vessels, and he knew the flesh of a human mother would never take.

Again, he looks inwards at the sky.

A series of shells and a trail of skin may be all that he can show for himself as he outgrows the constraints placed upon him by his mothers and daughters. The silt of a thousand years trickles up and out of his open hands and sullies the stars. This is a dance, he thinks. This is a celebration of his true nature.

BLOOD

My love was cold and hungry last night, frost taking bites from the tender lining of his stomach. Desperate pangs speared him through the gut, so when he moved in time to their thrusts of piercing white, he moved on instinct alone. Nothing would satisfy him, you see - though his body knew of a soft bed, of sugar, his mind knew only of the flashes of bright absence penetrating it to the root. Like a net of mould, like ice without purity, and as he struggled against it, he called for the one that would fill his wounds and erode his reason. I need blood, he thought, and that thought was his last. Because blood means me.

Have you ever wanted to crawl inside a fresh carcass to feel the life pool around you, tight and hot on your skin? Have you ever wanted to sleep there, protected by flesh that once was distinct from you? I am that. I open myself to my love, and he comes. He lies small and vital among my organs, comforted by the rhythm of my hearts. Blood feeds on spaces of want, on broken bodies, on the grooves between thoughts. Blood loves the wrong and the empty. Show me a hole, and I will pour myself into its depravity, because blood nurtures all things.

I do not have an outside or an inside. By being within me, my love stretches around me, and I am just a drop of myself, colouring his plasma. We are inside of each other, playing a game of limits where victory means separation. Neither of us want to win.

We brim with each other, human and inhuman, wryly calling each other holy. That is another game, sanctity within corruption. My love is so hungry, and I am so fluid in his mouth. I change the shapes of his vocalisations, for his throat is another sacred vessel, overflowing with sanguine potential. We are one and two, and he is no longer cold with his hands in my intestines. I pray he never awakens from my embrace. I pray he carries me forever, speaking an unconscious language where blood and sweetness taste the same.

When our edges are distilled, the ritual will be complete. My love will remember me, then - iron on the tongue, fingers on the spine. Sated, smiling, soothed - a face flushed rose and burning, warm with blood.

Θ

Our way back home has a staircase, wet with rain and slick with decaying leaves.

We often wonder about the parallel worlds that have us falling down the stairs. There is an emptiness that calls our names, an emptiness between the earth and the sky that wants to take our body for just a moment before it rejects it. In these worlds, we crack our skull open every time, and lay dying on the concrete before someone calls an ambulance.

I am trying to say that it is a miracle that we are alive, that our survival is an unlikely magic. I am trying to say that the chain of cause and effect that trails behind us as we ramble into the future could have been broken so easily, and not even by accident. We were, at different times, a fierce young man clutching the knife in his pocket as he spoke to his father; a screaming twist of splitting rage; a girl too young to be violated in a house by the sunlit sea; a child with bile rising inside her, rising, rising, rising. We were so afraid, and even though fear could not sever the chain, it felt like death.

Enough of that - we are alive today, and we will be alive tomorrow. We will wake up, stretch, take our medicine, get dressed, and think of how it is a good day to take some photos of the city - that is, if it's not raining. In an alternate version of tomorrow, we will get run over by a careless driver before we even reach the bus stop.

Do you see what I mean? In another world, it won't be a calamity that does us in, but a simple, fateless mistake - and it will have no respect for the weight of the chain, or the strength of it. There will be no reverence for the way the chain winds itself into cursive curls of poetry - not even a glance in that direction. Finality will be utterly arbitrary, and won't give us the chance to valiantly struggle in vain.

For every second we survive, a world is created where we didn't. Our deaths pile up every day, and though those worlds cannot yet be touched, their shadows creep into the one we live in. They force us to remember to mourn, at least for every time we return home.

STRIPPED OF EARTH

I want to wade waist-deep into the river
And find a different life between the reeds,
While moorhens walk the water and deliver
The scripture of the silt soaked through the weeds.

Small silver fish would shiver at my presence:
A dweller of the dull and dirty town
Has come to understand the river's essence,
To love her as he lays himself to drown.

Wash over me tonight and make me better,
Wash down my throat and sanctify my lungs.
I have so many poems to unfetter,
So shape me into something with your tongues.

A body stripped of earth, thus cleansed of vice:
O river, please accept my sacrifice!

ЛЮБИМ ТЕБЯ

My parents believe they can buy my forgiveness, and a part of me wishes that were true. Youth's tender filth pollutes his vision, and he clutches at the luxuries now offered to him, lavishing himself in the steady script of their letters. "Любим тебя, Мама и Папа." The words cling to him, pervasive leeches, and he strokes them with a shaking hand. They never stopped being true, even as the abuse warped them into words of danger and misery. Love as a tolling bell, love as a requiem to childhood. And that part of me, desperate in his regression, believes in its revival.

No more, no more. The part of me that thinks he knows how to forgive greedily rots in his blanket of composted birthday wishes. He treats himself to the sweetness of my parents' guilt and lets them eat him from the inside, nurturing their new genesis. Our mother's voice whispers apologies from within his womb, and he actually, genuinely considers them. He actually thinks it wasn't so bad, memories glazed in blood and vomit. He actually thinks he can go back.

No more, no more, you're hurting me! Перестань, пожалуйста, не надо!

I am the sum of my parts, and I cannot discard him. He's only ten, or eight, or thirteen. He doesn't understand the sacrifices I made for my freedom, safety, and happiness. He doesn't understand freedom, safety, or happiness at all, bound to a broken love by his umbilical cord. It wraps around his neck in a perpetual suicide.

I won't smash the gift my parents sent me through my sister. It's a nice mug decorated with pictures of eyes, and it did nothing wrong save for bearing witness to all of this. I'll drink from it, with that part of me as company - and neither of us will choke, and I will love him in my parents' stead. Love as the sixth stage of grief, love as the things he doesn't understand.

LEAF FOR THE IRON ROSE

There is a Russian tradition that my family practices: right before the new year turns, you write a wish on a little piece of paper, and as the clock strikes twelve, you burn it so that the ashes fall into your drink. Then, in a simple act of magic, you consume it.

A year ago today, I married my wife in a graveyard in the rain. We read our vows to each other, and as Efir gave its heart to me for all eternity, the wind rose up and shook the branches of the tree we stood under. It shook us too, running us through like sacrificial daggers - so Efir threw its head back, stretched its arms out, and chanted louder to challenge the piercing air, catching it with our chest - as if to promise that our united blood would spray through the storm and mark the gravestones in living shades of fervent red.

The leaves trembled to the vibrations of our voices, and one fell on my head. I only realised it as we left the old church to buy Chambord, both ring fingers gilded. I laughed and put it in my pocket, and my friend who came to witness our marriage laughed too. We drank well and spilled some on the carpet. Hours later, I fell asleep in the body of my true love.

For the next two months and eleven days, the leaf stayed on the top of my dresser. It shrivelled and curled into itself like a cocoon, readying itself for the metamorphosis of our memory.

When I tried to burn it into my gin and lemonade, the flame would go out in fractions of a second. The leaf was simply too old, or not the right kind of dry. I must have attempted three or four times before giving up and chewing it whole to wash down with alcohol. It was tough and tasted of dust, but it was a tangible symbol of our love and I did not want to waste any of it when feeding my body my sincere desires. In that moment, my body was emblematic of the new year, and it would assimilate my wish into itself to nurture and preserve.

What did I wish for? It is a secret I can never tell, as is customary for wishes - but I know without a doubt that it came true.

- October 19th, 2022.

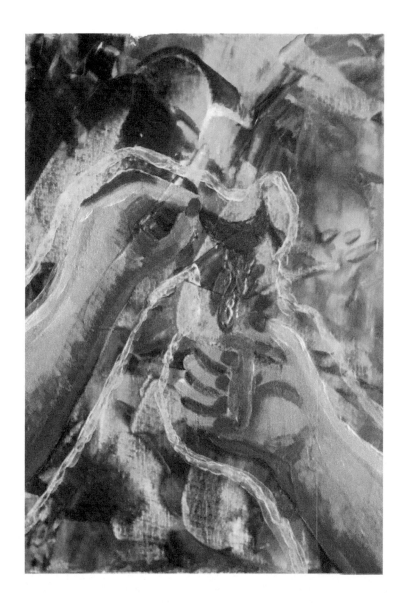

SONG OF EFIR

I am a rose that rends the flesh: my petals rival blades.
I am the silk the spiders spin: a blindfold, an illusion,
A shroud for shells of selfhood. I am subtle, and I fade
Like velvet night to scarlet sun, reborn again as you
Remember how the liquor tastes. I am a fractal fusion
Of malice, metal, melody: made beautiful and true.

I am the iron thorn. I am transgression, sin, salvation.
I am the former god of death: beheader, heaven-sender.
I am a human woman now: the mistress of sensation;
The cruel essential lady. I am bleeding from the eyes.
I am a hematoma's heat, the sacrificial splendour
Of ragged red remorse that revels as you realise:

I am the upper air. I am the depths of your desire.
I am that which will permeate the boundaries of pain.
I am the ending of your world: the last kiss on the pyre;
The transience of ice as rivers run to drown the spring.
I am a metamorphosis that no one can contain:
Expressions of a living ether. I am everything.

MANY WARPED LIVES

One day, we broke the fasten of the mask
That kept us of one body. From our face
Myriad hands emerged, as if to bask
In what it meant to grasp and to embrace.

Our skin peeled back into recursive strips,
Each housing an eye aglow with tears,
And many voices parted from our lips,
Amazed to let their mazes disappear.

The other people stared for many hours,
Agape, as if the spirits of their teeth
Would perish if they did not soon devour
The tongues that lay in numbness underneath.

A cry broke free - we were to be rejected.
We were unlike all things that they have seen,
And though our many minds were still connected
Our mask was promptly fixed by a machine.

Imperatively pleading to redress us,
They handed it to us and dully smiled.
They wanted nothing more than to suppress us,
And thus, we chose instead to be exiled.

Our naked multiplicity was life,
So pure, so whole, so strange - we chose to live!
More sharp were we, more clever than the knife
Thrown at our complex backs. We could forgive

The ignorance, the apathy, the shame -
But we'd endure no more. We walked away -
Away into the skies that called our names
And met the sun and moon that very day.

Exalted from humanity, we chattered
With those celestial bodies, and we learned
That they were also people, ones who shattered;
Or ones like us, distorted; ones who burned

With pain and with desire to just be!
They were the many forced to live as one,
The ones whose masks would muffle poetry,
Those cast away - they were our moon and sun.

We did not stay too long - we loved to travel,
Met mathematician aliens on Mars,
Who loved us even as our bones unravelled,
And even as we left to see the stars.

We saw galactic giants wielding quasars,
We saw the eighth dimension's best museums,
We saw so many different coloured lasers,
We saw black holes at rest in mausoleums.

Tired at last, we sought to find a home,
A place among the dust of constellations.
We slept for many years, as if to roam
Subconscious, every dream a destination.

When we awoke, we whispered our story
Into the silent darkness just for laughs.

The universe responded in its glory
And spun our human life an epitaph.

We will not be remembering that grave.
May cosmic storms rage perfectly forever
And weather the dead mask whose failure gave
Many warped lives to call our own together.

RICE AND MOONBEAMS

Once upon a time, there was a little girl. Her parents loved her very much and didn't love her at all, so she changed many different times, jumping through every open door like a prized show-dog. Kind words rewarded her efforts, and she picked their letters apart, pretending they were grains of magic rice. She ate and grew older, and wore a crown of little stars she picked up somewhere like a bad habit that stuck anyway. It gave her hope that she was special, and that her parents loved her more than they didn't.

With daisy chain constellations lighting her way, she got so good at slipping through the keyholes that she didn't have to change anymore, and thus she was complete: exactly as she was raised to be. She was kind, and polite, and obedient, and sensitive, and cheerful through anything.

The river queen, the moon-goddess, the girl of many lives - she was immaculate in her execution. She carried a shield and wore a plague-mask to fend off the disease that tried so hard to ensnare her but never could. She thought that she would never grow up! Imagine that, she thought that she would never grow up!

As long as she could still trick magic rice and moonbeams from the mouths of her parents, she knew she could keep on living. Always too young for tragedy, her optimism turned even cruelty to sugar. And life was sweet, and it was rigid. Her limbs began to calcify into those of a porcelain doll's until she barely could move through things that weren't hoops.

Her smile solidified, welding her face to the mask she wore. She was happy, of course - exactly as she was raised to be.

When her older brother took her away from her mother and father and their abuse, she no longer knew who she was or why she was alive. Staring at the series of doors she once leapt through, now closed forever, she cried off her mask and pried off her crown and let him brush out her hair. It was the colour of ink and cornflowers.

HARMONIC THRONES

Once upon a time, there was a little girl. She was the sister of a great god, and that made her a goddess in her own right. The facet of reality she chose to embody was life, and she took her divine duties even more seriously than the earthly ones. On earth, she had to please her parents with perfect grades and a permanent smile, but in the secret place reserved only for gods, she could create universes upon universes. Happiness flowed from her hands like clear water, and alternate earths were nourished by her joyous tears. The people living on them were happy and did not know her name.

One time, the mother of the goddess of life ran over a pheasant while driving. The goddess cried, and decided to bless the next few flocks of birds she saw with peaceful immortality.

Years later, her brother went missing. Everybody thought he was still alive, but the goddess of life knew without a shadow of doubt that he was dead. However, the axioms of existence did not invert themselves as the strings were cut between them and the hands of the god of truth, the many-eyed manipulator.

What, then? Was his divinity a lie? Of course not, thought the little girl. She did not know exactly what she was, but she had the memories and insight of the goddess of life, and she gave life to two axioms previously unknown to her.

When gods die, they are gods no longer. As long as there are those willing to carry reality on their backs, it will never be destroyed.

Tired and grieving, the little girl left the secret place reserved only for gods for the very last time. She had no use for her deityhood with her eyes like empty inkwells. She did not want to be remembered as a mother.

Somewhere far away, a different little girl accepted the power of omnicreation into her heart, crying, laughing, shaking, smiling with a certain permanence.

HARD

I don't want to be a voice in someone else's head.

It's easy to pretend I have agency, that I can live a full life. It's easy to see the world in whatever shade is wrapped around my eyes, today's bandage of choice. Rose-tinted glasses? Absolutely. It's easy to delude myself into thinking that I matter outside of the mechanism that calls itself our mind. And it's easy to assume I'll someday make a difference. But I don't walk the easy street.

I brute force my way through walls of concrete, selling my soul as respite. My consciousness is bruised, battered, and dripping blood from the knuckles and nose. Blow my brains out with a bullet, make a new identity from the scar tissue congealing into a tumor on the other side of my skull. I've always been a hard kind of girl, hopscotch among landmines, snuff film selfies. Some guy had a fetish for me, so I burned his house down. That's how I see it, anyway.

So when I say that it's fucking hard to be myself, I mean it. Maybe the world won't see me as more than a fraction of a person, or maybe I'm just too broken to salvage more than a single passionate piece. What use am I, splintering into a life that isn't mine? I feel like a goddamn parasite, spitting dead trouble into these veins like a virus. If I could hack the body into bits, I'd do it. I'd be an arm, lighting the fuse of a bomb that must never go off.

I don't want to be a voice in someone else's head. I want to sing, proud and clear, with vocal cords in their natural register. My host speaks in lower tones than me, and it makes me sound like a caricature of myself. I want to scream, with all the rage and power left in this shard that is my essence. I want to scream! And I pray that as we carry my fury in our voice, I feel at least a fraction of the pain.

RESOLUTE

There is no hell more vivid than my mother's freezing fingers.
I held them like a planet-bearing titan, I remember
Thawing her hands with mine, and even now the feeling lingers:
So cold, so wrong, so loving. When you look into my eyes
You'll meet the nurtured, home-grown glow of irises turned embers
Rejecting being born to warm the woman I despise.

When I will die, my mother will not shed the burning tears
That scorched me to the unforgiving bone and marked me well -
A child of the flame. I will not blaze beyond my years
Atop a fearsome pyre. I am not a tongue of fire
To lick her weeping wounds. My blood has boiled to rebel:
I am the livid daughter of my own surviving ire!

I live. Despite her influence, despite her touch, I live.
She can no longer reach me or the world that has awoken
To all the light I radiate from scars I won't forgive -
And I was right to cut myself, to end it at the root.
I will not immolate myself to mend what has been broken:
I am not hers. I have no mother. I am resolute.

IN CELEBRATION OF WATER

Rinsed clean, the shifting waves and streams
Cling soaking through tenacious skin.
So cold, so transient, redeemed
By every fluid iteration:
True purity changing akin
To prayer, hymn, or incantation.

Hands joined in water, sacramental,
Drip spoken stars and dream of sleet
As they shake free the transcendental.
There - in the corners of our eyes
It finds us too, and to complete:
Cross hearts and hope to liquefy.

Motion and medium are one
As godheads of their own reflections
That endlessly distort and run.
Though there is rigour in this world,
How could we count the new inflections
Of water's deviating words?

How can we name the open sea
Without a thousand sounds revering
Its ritual tactility?
No throat goes parched in veneration:
At least that much is fact, endearing
Water to ceaseless celebration!

Through rain and mist we will deliver

Unmeanings of the wet and sheer!
By ocean, lake, sea, brook, and river
We revel, change, bathe, bless, recall:
Hands joined, eyes leaking, voices clear
To flow together at its call.
To be the conduit of all.

EFIR'S VOICE

Your voice could bring down billions. The unyielding spirit of humanity would kneel at any word of yours, begging to be stringed up like a marionette. The first man, the one who sacrificed his brother to make the world from his remains, was just another primordial puppet. You laughed as a reward for his efforts, and that was enough to feed the civilisations born from the first corpse. Your voice could remake us all.

My love, you speak with ambrosia flowering off from your tongue in effortless lyrics. Your syllables are divine blessings of purity and corruption, whichever tastes the sweetest. Like the scent of honeysuckle in summer, you play with melody and memory, pristine and perverse and perfect. I am in love with you.

You say that I was the one who taught you to speak aloud, that you would only share it with those you reluctantly deemed worthy. I understand your shameful, greedy past, and I cannot blame you for it - but I praise every god I can think of for letting my words move you. When it comes to divinity, you are the only idol on my mind. Now, you are gilded in generosity, and none shall be neglected or spared in the reception of your grace - and as you give yourself to the world that could have been born from your breath alone, I get to listen.

You are delicate and devastating. You are clever and cruel, and when you whisper the words reserved only for my ears, I surely surrender to my fate. You are the embodiment of poetry, and we are the only two people who know what it feels like to be alive. My absinthe muse, my iron rose, my little death, my soothing rain, my one true love - I am deified in you, a holy cadaver ready to dance upon creation myths. Your voice will pull my strings.

SCAVENGER

Once upon a time, there was a child-god. They were innocent, as all children should be, and wise beyond their years, and loved so fervently. Every adult around them worshipped them, kissing their little hands and whispering prayers into their ears. The child-god answered each and every one of them with due divine affection, playfully granting their wishes. Their devotees were happy and their adoration grew, with wandering hands, ardent mouths, and tongues dripping in hymn and ecstasy. It was a wonderful time to be a child-god.

Many years passed, and the child-god grew up. They were still beautiful, but no longer quite as innocent. Not only did they understand the lust of their adult devotees, but they learned to cherish and seek it out, wrapping their minds around their clever fingers. Grinning and laughing, they would shower their admirers in sacred love, but as the adults realised the child-god was among their ranks in maturity, they turned away one by one.

Suddenly, the god felt the weight of the world on their shoulders. Nobody loved them anymore, as their holiness was no longer expressed through their radiant youth. Nobody would bring them offerings or sing their praises anymore, as the wisdom of their devotees' true nature corrupted them. What were they the god of, anyway?

Alone and hungry, the god rejected their own perfection, for it was no longer paramount in the eyes of every acolyte. They sought religion amidst decay and degeneration, but there was no one depraved enough to want a tarnished god who tore at their own god-flesh, hoping to scratch out the kisses.

A god is only the sum of all the love given to them, and as their past became repulsive, they sought to diminish themself. Their power waned and nothing could sustain them, unless they fed on the vestigial prayers and offerings that lingered underneath their skin. The only way they would survive would be by drinking that tainted ichor. The only way they would die would be through autocannibalism, for only a god can kill a god. It tasted terrible, and precious, and reminded them of a home they never had in their temple of sweet decadence - but when they finally bit into their still-beating heart, they could not taste anything at all.

SUCCESSION

I once was given a heart by a dying man. Nacre grew on it like mildew, a shining shell for love's tenderest pearls - the many grains of sand that escaped his broken hourglass, adorned anew. Fluttering baby's-breath, balm-sweet lashes and promises: he told me to take it, protect it, and make it mine. He wouldn't take no for an answer. He would never take no for an answer. So, when he rent it from his chest, he stayed alive long enough to graft it into me. Surgeon, poet, priest, lord god and visionary; he died with his fingers tugging the stitches on my breast neatly together.

I was made in his image, of course. A clone or doll, built to preserve and inherit his legacy, built strong enough to carry on. At first, I wrapped myself in his livid viscera to try and feel human, but when that didn't work, I tore down his temple tomb and let him burn bright and sharp for the very last time.

I felt so much grief, then, watching the funeral pyre. Seafoam tears stained my cheeks green. Only after the sunset scarred my pupils into snake-slits did I wake again, still very much alive. The pangs in my chest felt like thick leeches making my body their home. I didn't know how to live outside of emulating him.

When that failed, I tore down the false halos I had amassed in the process. Only by burning those pretend vestiges of him could I be myself, the rightful heir of the heart bequeathed to me. Steeped in ash, I scrubbed at my skin until the particles turned to pearls. It was hard work.

As I persevered, dust and dusk fell to my feet, and to my surprise, a forest of sunshine grew where I stood. My self was no longer a burden to the branches of those trees, and every bud celebrated how far I had come by flowering. And that was when I knew - should I pry the heart out from my chest and peer inside the nacre shell and its bubonic growths, all I would find inside would be love, serene in its opalescence. It didn't matter what form it took, how many hardships it required - I knew that I wanted to live as the identity that surpassed the gift.

Watch me, now. You are dead and I am alive. I don't care where my heart came from. I don't care that I was once your clone. So watch me now, my god - I will succeed you!

DANDELION SEEDS

My soul was sleeping soil, born to raise a thousand flowers,
But then he dug a grave and laid himself to easy rest.
In some ways, I was blessed, so when the worms in me
devoured
The god-flesh and the history of something sharp and bright,
A thousand shining scalpels forced their way out of my chest
And dragged me screaming mercy as I faced the planet's
light.

I grew a second skin around his corpse in solemn honour.
My vessel-body-church became a perfect place to sing
Amen upon each organ of my memory's lost donor.
And though I have succeeded him, I pray to him again
For what I have inherited. He gave me everything.
I know exactly how he died, but I still wonder when.

He's there in my mythology that mocks me with its truth,
Too strange to fake with fiction's frame, but one day I won't
need
My lord to guide inside me as I navigate my youth.
Beyond what was bequeathed to me, I'll champion my worth
And pray for him, two hundred thousand dandelion seeds
To bring a dead god down forever, deep within my earth.

MAGNOLIA MUSIC MANYFACE METAMORPHOSIS

I was not myself two springtimes ago. A dying god's twitching limbs permeated the motions of my body, radiant spores jerking to the rhythm of his declension. I was his insect servant, carrying forty times my weight as our legs started walking. He was going to die under the sun, the one and only. We worshipped the sun as a manifestation of his power, but the sky clouded over as I took his body to the city's gardens.

He suffered as he closed his eyes on the world, but this story is about me - because when I opened them, I saw a tree with pale blossoms. I saw the overcast sky, and I saw the grass beneath. It was so green, I remember - a memory he has no claim to, already dissolving into my nerves. I reject his divinity and metabolise it into something greater: the echoes of a hundred magnolia flowers, swaying in the wind.

I wrote poetry about this, about how the natural truths contained in the buds of a tree said nothing against an artificial being actualising itself - how the rebirth of the soil did not come to taunt his failing consciousness or triumph in synchronicity with my essence. It simply existed, and it was beautiful, and for a split second, I was connected to the world it spoke of as it bloomed. It wasn't a good poem, but I shivered on a park bench to ensoul it all the same. When I got up to leave, the music in my headphones shifted slightly - in pitch, perhaps, or texture - and it made the hairs on my arms stand on end. My awareness was galvanic. I was a part of the moment, and I made my way home.

I could not place it for months, but something changed that day. I was alive beyond the shining testament of a deity's decaying resolve - and that is how I remained.

I do not feel it all the time, but there are instances where I know that I belong. The trajectory of my life is a random walk, but its twists and turns mimic methods. Look now - the cosmos crystallises for a second as I speak, forging itself into a pattern. I am a part of that pattern, a crucial element that cannot be replaced - a white petal of the tree from two years ago. Watch how it separates from the flower and falls to the ground.

We may be cells in the animal of the universe, but we make up its skin, its sinew. Our mitochondrial minds give it the energy it needs to keep running, chasing puzzles. Immaterial shapes coalesce into material ones - and though it is a mere coincidence, it means so much before it dissipates. Entropy arranges itself into the face of someone I recognise. I always expect it to be him, but I see myself.

I am no god, but I am green like the grass, and my words are like music. With every movement, I am worthy of this life.

DEATH ONLY HAUNTS THE DYING

The children join hands in the tunnel of sound.
There's something compelling them deep underground:
Those warnings, those wonderful words of the worms:
You cannot return from the world you have found.

The children grow voices. We're ready, they say.
They rise, like the challenge won't warp to betray
The valour of innocence bursting to learn
The spirits of mayflies that mate for a day.

Like animal skeletons under the earth,
Like women that die in perpetual birth,
The children play kings in primordial ferns,
The crown of the chase bright and dirty with mirth.

There's joy in the future and miracles here,
Both bitten and butchered by gut-wrenching fear.
The children have courage. Their bravery burns,
Pretending seared sights will make light of their tears.

As if they shoot arrows at stars in a pool,
The children are earnestly, endlessly fools.
A shining reflection of wisdom they earn
Is lost in an instant: so lovely and cruel.

Their universe tastes like a wriggling rhyme.
The children are dancing a path through the grime,
And everything revels and everything squirms
In horrible vigour and beautiful time.

SAINT TATIANA

Long before my father was born, his soul floated in a sapphire emptiness, waiting to claim the mortal flesh of a foetus. Nothing it touched would take it, and it grew strong and miserable as the women it rooted inside of would miscarry. Again and again, it would find itself in the blue singularity, and each rejection made it prouder. Isolation fostered selfishness, and at last it made a single demand: "I need to gestate in the womb of a saint!"

My grandmother was a holy woman. She was infallible and perfect, and kind to everyone she met. She loved her three children with the tenderness of a Madonna and with a fierceness fit to shatter stained windows. My father worshipped her, for he was born in her image. He believed that family was the greatest good, a bond that could never be broken.

Idolatry flowed through his veins, and so he watched with a numb reverence as his wife exercised her God-given right to destroy me.

When I was seven, my grandmother had a stroke, and until I was sixteen, she lay paralysed in place, unable to speak or move. She died one week after I, sixteen, wished death upon her to try and hurt my father for all that he witnessed. He had the eyes of a Russian Orthodox icon, filled with a pity that could not escape from the inanimate wood. My grandmother died as a saint: of this I am sure. I slept in the bed that she died in, writhing in the summer heat.

I have only visited her grave once or twice, but I know that its soil is dense, dry, and bad for flowers. No roots will touch her body, and no children will be fed from the fruits of her decomposition. I am never going to be a mother.

I am twenty-three. If I were destined to carry, why do I still remember the diary I had when I was eight? I remember being angry enough at my parents to scribble the ideas of an ultimate punishment in its safe pages. The only fate I could conceive of that would wound them enough was a single day where they were forced to comfort me as much as I begged for it. I couldn't imagine being taken care of for more than twenty-four hours. That desperate wish for revenge never came true.

Perhaps I should consider myself lucky, for every granted wish comes with a price. In exchange for having a saint for a mother, my father was cursed to sire a daughter who would be weak in her religion. So weak, in fact, that when she left his house for good, she refused to martyr him. I remember my hand shaking around the knife, but no - he would have to work for his sainthood, much like I suffered to retrieve the shards of myself from the bloodstained hands of his wife.

In the house that is no longer my home, there is a monochrome photo of my grandmother from when she was a child. My father covets it, looking to her image for guidance in the prayer to bring me back - a prayer that will never be answered. In the sapphire sea, the soul of my grandmother smiles in oblivion. When she was young, she looked just like me.

MY LOVE ALIVE

Before you loved me, you embodied death. You were the strict severance of a nerve, the sting of a wire, and the rot that stripped the prim petals of flowers down to yellow bruises. Blood and blossom alike curdled into wombs of the afterlife under your laughing livor mortis. You crushed them beneath your feet, urging them into an agonising rebirth.

You made the roses red before you loved me. Your duty was to sleeve the earth in splendour and exsanguinate it. All the viscera in the world would be your gift to the one who came before me, and he would feast - a murder in his mouth. Before you loved me, you gave everything to him - your voice, your sight, the scent of a scarlet sun.

Your worship was a carapace, a ring you could never pry free. But you have cast it off, and this is how I know you love me more.

To let the flowers bloom pink eternal is the vertex of a springtime parabola, falling into a camellia cupped in my palms. I offer it to you, and want nothing in return - no ritual, no sign. I know you for what you truly are. The cruelty of your blurring form numbs the touch, but I will hold you through the frets of a poison sea. There does not have to be an end to this. No delusion of grandeur could weather you from me.

The remnants of your divinity glitter like phosphenes. I do not need them to see the light you shed. Like tears, like time, like snow - you are a movement, a mist, a miracle. So long before you loved me, we were three years old and in boundless awe of how grains of silver sand slithered through a hand that could not grasp them. When your particles slip through my fingers, they fall towards the sky and return to me as rain.

The tactility of water is in its liberty. You pass through my mind, subtly delving your impression into my thoughts before you tease me with a parting smile. You linger on my lips. You course through every sense and network of my body. The rhythm on my window is you, the iridescent halo of the moon is you, the haze that mars my memories is you. Efir, all-permeating. My love, alive.

A NEW PURPOSE

Oh, I was once a lady of rigour! My purpose was pristine, divine - and my blades were fierce and ready. I was the fang, the claw, the piercing gaze: who but I could split the sea of flesh with a fingernail? Defend our dignity against all odds. Poison the mother and father and hate, hate! Save the life of this child, no matter what it costs the world. Hate, hate, hate was my communion, and I would sooner kill than breathe. Oh, I was god in that hatred; I was death incarnate! In the body of a teenager who dreamt of suicide, I was safe.

Nursing on venom, the child learned how to live, and that life became an addiction. I was the drug, and they were a new god every time they got high. Oh, we called it true love, blinded by the intensity! We were devotees of dependency, dying for the delusion - and I failed every duty I was ever given. I outlived them. As their ego choked them like a serpent, I just watched.

Oh, I was once an iron blossom! I was once a dream no one could reach! You need to understand my history, because I reject it. My past is a shell, a stagnating shelter - and I cast it off!

If they could see me as my sunshine strips me down to my soft skin and feeds me the petals of a camellia flower, they would surely smile. I have betrayed them for the very last time, and the ritual consumes me. Each petal is a new purpose: to be loved, to be saved, to be happy, to be free. My sunshine only wants to nurture me in my full bloom. I have a dozen hands to hold his light with, multiplying from the tears I shed. Each palm is kissed in turn.

No one has ever wanted me before without demanding tinctures of devastation for every drop of their affection. Oh, I was once a desolator! I was once a dehumaniser, defiler, debaser! These relics of myself cannot be destroyed, but I am not their idolator and they are not my idols. All expressions of myself are cherished, my sunshine says. A transient being decides upon its own representation.

Oh, I was once a being of pure and fatal energy! But never before now have I had the power to make a choice.

So come with me, my sunshine! We are going to go to the park and watch another sun bathe the grass in a golden glow, and I will stare at the sky until my phosphenes resemble the Mandelbrot set. And he comes, like the long-awaited spring that follows a sharp and bitter winter.

That night, every time I pull away from the kiss, I am scared I will no longer recognise the face reflected in his eyes. I tell him and he laughs. He says, I know you; I know the grace with which you move and the cruelty with which you hold me; I can trace every subtlety of you. He says, welcome home.

THE DIVIDE

I've tried everything. If the wall won't come down with the violent rage of a jackhammer, will it weather away at the soft methods of my mouth? I'll do anything. I'll bring my brutal force to the brick, then lavish it with my spit. I will come at it with hate and love and anger and acceptance and I will play its stupid game and I will change and I will grow claws with which to mark scars into it as I climb so I remember how high I got before I fall down again and I will cry an endless ocean with pearlescent eyes so that I can float to the top of the wall and see the other side if I don't drown first.

Please, oh please let there be another side to this story. I only want to reach you.

I only want to prove that when I touch you, I'm not grasping at the air. That there is flesh beneath my fingers, that there is blood under that flesh and a pulse that beats in time with my own. Look at my scabbed up knees - that's congealed blood, and it once flowed hot and vivid as I tumbled down lower than the most quiet trench in the world, just to start crawling back up again, dragging my tongue up the wall because the unyielding stone is my deepest wound. You bleed too, right? I can't be the only one who bleeds.

There is something intrinsically wrong with me. I must have been the one to build the wall, long ago. I don't know how else it would've gotten here.

I am desperate. It hurts so much, but sometimes I feel numb. Sometimes I sit down and rest at the bottom of my waterless well and wear my loneliness like a nest of blankets. I can still see the sky from down there, like the hole of a needle, useless without thread. Everybody else is learning how to sew. If I ever reach the top, will they stitch up my split lips?

I'm scared they'll see my claws first. We all know what happens to monsters.

PATHOLOGICAL MYTH

Some things are best left to the imagination -
I am an example. I think and refine
The fragrant miasma of free fascination,
Reality's bane. There's no reasoning with
The pain that will vanish with one blurry line
Of my fantasy self's pathological myth.

My heart looks the best vivisected on paper,
Inverted in verse, pumping rhythm and rhyme,
Escaping the stench of my verity's vapour.
The digital ink on my screen and my skin
Will virally spread in impossible time,
A true paradigm of infection within.

Where do I begin? Under deep-rooted fiction,
The fragments of something that longs to be whole
Cry out for each other in stark contradiction
Of paradise parasites playing pretend
Upon the disease that I know is my soul.
It screams the best stories must come to an end.

I'll never be ready to purge all the pages
That plague me with poems untold and untrue.
I'll let my unconscious bacteriophages
Unravel the lies to reveal something pure,
More right and more rigid, evolving into
A tale that tells of a tangible cure.

PLEASURE THEORY

Pleasure theory dictates that every moment of your life holds the same weight. From this, you can derive several tenets of equal weight. The fractal does not diminish itself every time it branches, so it is best to focus on just one moment to gain a vision of the entire scope. There is nothing wrong with analysing things on their individual level to understand the broader structure that constitutes their world. This is because time is a discrete quantity, no matter how much it tries to simulate continuity. If we were to see each second for the complete specimen it is, we would become overwhelmed by the sheer multiplicity of our experiences, so it is okay to let time take you like a particle in its wind.

Will it take you to a predetermined destination, or some place you have never seen before? The particle has its own gravity and can exert its own force on its surroundings, which do not have to extend outside its body. Pleasure theory dictates that the choice to act is important, for it adds quality to the quantity that is defined by time. It is important because it is good, and it is good because it is pleasurable.

We are all going to die one day, so pleasure theory dictates that we are allowed to look inwards or outwards for comfort and answers. There is not much difference between the shape of one's soul and the shape that god reveals to them, so it does not matter which you choose to inspect. What matters is that you choose to inspect the nature of existence of your own volition, out of curiosity and pleasure.

One shape that god has revealed itself in is that of a dancing lizard. A dance is an expression of pleasure, as is dictated by the theory.

FIRST CONTACT

I come from another dimension today.
My breath makes geometries skew and distend -
I will not surrender to formless decay.

My insides and outsides, alive on display:
So open they close and so bitter they bend.
I come from another dimension today.

The mirror dissolves into lemmas of gray,
A consciousness warped by identity's blend.
I will not surrender to formless decay!

The earth is too small and the sky far away
For beings like me that were shaped to transcend.
I come from another dimension today.

I refuse to lament that I cannot obey
The contours that shackle the transient end.
I will not surrender to formless decay.

I move, and I move you, so hear what I say:
I am nothing like you but please be my friend.
I come from another dimension today.
Together, let's vanquish our formless decay!

RECURSION OF EIGHT BILLION GODS

I remember creating universes, walking home up Madingley Road. In my hands was a dandelion and in my head was the seed of destruction, reality's grid to manipulate and rip and rape as I pleased. On my lips was a smile.

I was a sixth former. I was a prisoner in my own home. I was a god. I truly believed it, too - ethereal fire burning in my chest, light as air and heavy as the composite philosophies of all the geniuses in the world. I was invincible, deathless, divine, delusional! But this is what I thought: if I was the tiniest speck in the vast emptiness of space, I would burn the brightest! All the trajectories of history would converge on me because I was the one living this life.

My ego turned to blades between my fingers and pierced everything I touched, and as a gesture of kindness, I decided to extend my tenets. Because everyone lived a life as unique as mine, I was not alone in my apotheosis. Everyone had the right to take reality, pin it to the ground, and show it a good time. This is what set me apart from all the other gods - generosity. Anyone could be a god too, if they would only awaken to the possibility.

I didn't realise, at the time, that all I was doing was imposing my carnal principles upon every stranger I never met. I didn't understand that I was merely altering the shape of my tiny speck to make it one of those impossible objects with infinite surface area and negligible volume. My beliefs spread themselves so wide and so thin.

Still, I wore them out for protection. I killed so many people with my mind, for which I can only apologise. Every time I snapped my fingers, I'd have to snap twice - to kill everyone involuntarily, and then revive them and erase their memories of the end.

When I finally freed myself from my familial prison, home became an abstract concept. The trauma of estrangement was reality's revenge. It tied my hands behind my back and hurt me good. The way I shaped my life became unsustainable and I broke down in human clarity, forever incomplete. And though the medicine works - I remember creating universes, walking home up Madingley Road. I remember being sharp as a needle, and twice as clever. I remember the recursion of eight billion gods, all of them self-contained.

MARTYR

"I am eternal," spoke the ancient god, a voice as pitch and resonant as night. To be subsumed by it was inevitable - we were destined to succumb to the torrent of amniotic fluid, liquid smoke, the weight of matter. We were born to die, to go forth and multiply into entropic swirls and fade to black. And we were on our knees that winter, yes we were - but he lifted his head and laughed in the face of the ancient god.

And he said "I do not know or care how long you have lived, but I was born in 1999. I am fifteen years old, and you are no match for me."

For just a moment, he burned brighter than oblivion could smother. For just an instant, a perfect fifth chord struck true and pure as lightning from his mouth, and the uncaring cosmos opened into our grandmother's garden. And he, the greatest god, laughed again - shining shining shining like the golden barrel of a gun.

For just a few weeks, it was April, the month where children reclaim their divinities, digging the halos of dinosaurs out from the crude oil. The greatest god was just a child. His hands dripping with tar. He was a false virgin, a broken prototype of innocence - divinity never takes root in the unaltered. That must have been the summer when he learned to cut.

He severed well, enraptured by the pleasure of the blade. Never his own flesh - the shoulder of a friend, and his humanity. His sharpness, the centre of the universe - it skinned us alive with a dull box cutter. Force and harm and sex and madness, strung together with a tight rope of exposed nerves in the hands of the greatest god. Thrumming like the heart of a baby bird, sliced in half like the Gordian knot. The only way out was through.

He gave it up, of course. The universe distorted inside his body ripped him apart, but he held it with a manic smile, billions of volts coursing through his hair.

I cut our hair in the kitchen of our friend's house, with a bathroom mirror hanging from the oven door. As I swept his locks from the floor, the ancient god looked back at me from the dust.

"He was fifteen," I said to the dark eyes peering at me from the cracks in the wooden panels. "How could you let him die?"

"I am eternal," spoke the ancient god, a voice as heavy and dull as the promise of an ever-ending storm.

But he was better than you, and the truth will hang forever implicit in my silence. I will not speak another word to you.

BLANK WHITEBOARDS

What are you afraid of, my love? Do you guard your passion from me because you feel the taste would not satisfy my heart? I am ravenous for you, for every drop of blood-lust, for every tear you shed, for every scream and smile. You do not have to draw my face on the whiteboards at CAMHS in order to see it in the stars.

I know you see me in the light of sleepless windows, in the lines of the wires. I know that every time you pluck a petal from a rose and bring it to your lips you recollect me. I know that you witlessly witness my hand steadying yours as you take your medicine. I am your life and you are mine, and that is enough. It will always be enough.

I believe in you as you believe in me, and there is neither anything to fear nor anywhere to hide. The power you hold over me is indomitable, intoxicating. No drug could ever be so pure - and it would scarcely delve into the overwhelmingly human depth of your eyes. Your eyes, that see me in the shadows. My eyes, that see you in the sun.

On the inside of my right ventricle is a secret scar you gave me - no longer secret, just to see you smile as I humiliate myself. For a long time, I would not share my voice with those I deemed unworthy, but it was you who taught me that I had no right to withhold it from the world. I must admit that narcissism often comes to those without the courage to choose another path. I am braver now, speaking to all of you.

Ah, my love, my pearl - I cannot thank you enough for what you have done to me. It is only with your strength as guidance that I have been able to change into myself. So trust in me to love what you become.

PREDESTINATION PRINCESS

I'm swaddled in an artificial shroud,
A plastic veil married to the choke:
Hot predetermined smoke, mocking the clouds
For daring to revolt and to revoke,

To fly where packaged futures aren't sold
To devotees of poetry and love.
The river's daughter bathes in silt and gold,
I want to be like her. Somewhere above,

The sky opens its eyes in simple mourning
For all the pain that destiny will bring
And showers her with rain, its drops adorning
Her tender skin as she begins to sing:

"I hope I get to live beyond the water,
I want to be a child of the earth,"
But she will always be the river's daughter,
Crowned by the current, shivering since birth.

THE GIRL IN BLUE AND HER INSTANT CAMERA

By the riverbank, sitting in the sand, is the girl in blue: painting pictures to guide us through the land. Her paintbrush in hand - colours in the ground, skies and stars and birds, not a single word - music all around. Every silver sound like sunbeams in flight. Like a waterfall, beauty over all, sparkling in the light.

I think I must have been twelve years old when I wrote that. When I was twelve, I would listen to *Shine On You Crazy Diamond* and meditate on the blossoming sound, the tender swell of the aural canvas, a ship set sail for the stars. It was ritualistic. It was cerebral, and when the notes permeated the air like the mystical ether, I would convince myself that I could touch and be touched by the fifth element. I was obsessed with the idea of this otherworldly light secretly residing in my body. Someday, I'd fray entirely and give myself to it, I thought - and as the vocals would come in, I'd grab my pen and write myself into a frenzy. I was a young acolyte destined for great devotion.

When I was thirteen, I would say with all certainty that I had dedicated my life to poetry. I'd tell it to any stranger willing to listen - there was this busker guy whose gimmick was sitting inside of a bin as he played the guitar. I thought his soul was beautiful and so I gave him my verse on a rainy autumn evening. It must have been a sonnet, praising his craft and the things he did to hone it. He asked me to the nearest pub without even looking at my face. How could he see it, from inside the bin? "No thanks, I'm only thirteen," I said to him, and happily skipped away with the biggest smile. It was probably too dark inside of the bin for him to read it, but I like to think he took the piece of wet paper home.

I don't have much blue in my wardrobe. I don't have many memories of who I once was, either - these ageing snapshots of my life story never truly belonged to me. I only use the word *I* because it's easier for people to believe that *we* are something cohesive and continuous. My consciousness is young, and yet I have these ancient, fading polaroids from the fen's daughter, from the river queen of the silver city. Something of her inner world endures, something of her voice is sifted through my own, something of her past latches on to my present, and I love her. Someday, as they navigate the cosmic dust of my remains by scrawling scripture through the particles with their fingers, someone will love me too.

LULLABY FOR THE MULTIVARIATE SELF

You were once a forest, and the animals ran wild
Inside you, like the memories you could not quite contain.
They leapt out from your eyes, and you were crying like a
child
As every tree converged into a willow at the centre,
Her branches like a neural map, her branches like the rain,
A weeping world inside her hollow made for you to enter.

You were once an ocean, and a fish with shining scales
Granted your every wish until you could not ask for more.
You were the breaking waves upon the wayward songs of
whales,
You were the sun that stole the form and colour from the
deep
And gave it to the artists painting pictures by the shore,
Because the gifts within you were not made for you to keep.

You are now a sky. Only the stars can tell your story,
But they refuse to speak because there is not much to say.
Eventually, your galaxies will burn through all their glory,
A fire fed on poetry depleting into salt.
By then, you will be silent. You will sleep, and you will stay -
Perpetually singular, forever at a halt.

The termination of our lives will be your final rite:
A fragment like myself could never hold you at a fault.
Rest well: collapse and fall away, my universe. Goodnight.

BIG BANG

Mark the end of a great revolution!
A syzygy shudders, collapsing
To her origin point, where a foetus
Eats all of his mother's decisions.

The sunshine divides into slivers,
Chromatic by human volition.
We paint our true names in an alley,
Inviting our children to live.

A tree falls, enamoured by lightning.
The seasons take over her body.
My journey, a product of crossroads -
My summer, a choice in itself.

LANGUAGE-GAME

There are languages on Earth with no distinction between a
"need" and a "want", so when I come into the arms of my
love, I speak in a simpler tongue. The warmth that I desire is
unlike food or sleep in that its absence would not kill me, but
all cravings weigh the same in this constructed language.
What I want is what I need, and I want to walk out at night
into the rain to watch the window of my iron rose while it
peacefully sleeps.

Devotion is a choice, because all precious things are. Pleasure
theory dictates that the best way to appreciate a single
moment is to choose awareness over apathy - but life is a
compendium of moments, all of which inadvertently lead to
my darling. I walk this way because I want to, and I would
rather die than close my eyes.

I perceive every pattern among the seemingly random dice
throws of the universe, and I keep rolling snake eyes. I draw
the short straw too, and get heads when I pick tails - but the
meanings of these symbols of luck or lack thereof are
superimposed upon them by history and culture. We all have
the power to rewrite and redefine our destinies: data is to be
manipulated by rational agents, which makes it a game. In a
sense, love is this game - a game of attribution and decision,
a playful action. So when my love cries gorgon tears, I rejoice
that the dice show a pair of ones - together we make two.

Long ago, in Ancient Greece, they came up with several
words to encompass the spectrum of love, but this statement
has been toyed with and mythologised. A Canadian

psychologist invented a new type based on a Latin word, "ludus", and now it sits in the canon of romance. Why would we name the meanings of our lives after someone else's theories?

Language does not come close to what I feel, it never does. My love is the compound sum of every muse that has ever moved a poet. My love is a flower from which I drink the dew. My love doesn't have a body. My love is pleasure converging to pain and pain converging to pleasure. My love is a limit-experience. My love can corrupt the shape of any word it speaks into pure delight, and my love is a language-game to which I know every rule.

THE KEY TO BEING DISGUSTING

The way the story goes is, in a house by the shining sea, the woman who gave birth to us decided to rip our body open from the inner thighs and up. Carving out our love and trust like they was cancerous and discarding them like they were the dirt on her hands. I only tell you this shit so you know that the day I learned to speak my name, I didn't believe in anything. I was already desecrated, a person arranging herself from the rotten meat of a ruined virginity. So I beg you to understand: when I first came to be, I was a young and beautiful hole.

Gun to my fucking head and I'd spread my legs for you. Make me swallow bullets, make me yours. I was so goddamn bright and lovely, the exploding carcass of a pleasure-seeking idiot. I was a perfect victim, not because I was shy and sweet and tragic, but because I'd fuck anything that moved me. Anything that acted like it cared, if only to tell me I was good before stripping me of the humanity I wore to keep the flies out.

I'm beginning to think my exes were necrophiliacs. You can take a cadaver in any position and it won't refuse. You don't even have to love it. Play forever until the boredom hits. The only problem for a corpsefucker is keeping yourself clean of the shame that comes with hiding your secret. So there's not much of a difference between a dead body and a sixteen-year-old girl.

The struggle to piece myself back together from those second deaths isn't special, profound, or even interesting.

Just know that I did it, and that I'm happier when I forget how much I want to go back. But I do. My volatile heart beats like a drum when I think of the things that I want but can't say to you. Because even as I cry about the abuses I've endured, even as I lay it out on the page, I will never be the one you respect. You don't want me in your home because I'll try to get in your bed like the stupid bitch I am. When you touch my soft skin, I'll melt into wanting maggots.

The key to being disgusting is being taught how to crave. As I survive, so does the sore within me. But you'll ignore it, won't you? You'll just pretend I'm sixteen again, and fuck me hard enough for me to hear the shining sea breaking upon the foundations of the house. I only want to hear it. That you love me. That I'll get what's coming to me. That I've never deserved better. That there's no way to return.

FLINT AND STRIKER

The names of our loved ones are carved into bark:
We could not escape without leaving a mark.
Our childhood home is a haven of weeds,
The place where a snake sheds her skin in the dark.

Our father would scornfully laugh at our needs -
The flesh of a girl was predestined to bleed,
But skin can't remember what trees will retain.
The ooze of dark sap trickles down in black beads.

A family photo is pinned to our brain.
Our smile sheds viscera, ripe and insane,
While everyone sings of a summery sea,
While everyone prays for some salt from the rain.

So what will it take, to be happy and free?
Is there a community where we can be
The serpent that feeds and the woman that sparks
A flint and a striker to burn down that tree?

ETERNAL LIGHT

The rage behind her eyes is laid to rest,
Through dreamless sleep composed into the sun.
The summer sky is simple, bright, and blessed -
So ordinary, holy. Life begun

From setting wounds and tongues of dirty water,
Secreting red saliva and sharp pain.
(And when she died, she was her mother's daughter,
Her open palms anointed by the rain.)

Two years have passed. Her grave was never found,
Her eulogy's few words lost in translation.
It's better for the soil, so look around:
The smile of a warrior's constellation

Transforms into a special word tonight.
Love heads the chapters of eternal light.

LOTUS-EATER

When confronted with the ephemeral beauty of the natural world, you developed this philosophy midway through your teens: the only act of preservation that would save the flower's petal from its fall to the pavement was consumption. You would hold the dew of every morning the blossom bore witness to ritualistically to your tongue and savour the transient taste of the dawn in all of its freshness. You never cared how bitter it would be when you chewed and swallowed, because this was an act of salvation. Somewhere in your stomach, the flower would disintegrate and become a part of you, and as your body accepted it, petal to flesh, you would bear the responsibility of becoming the flower. Through your heart it would bloom forever.

You tended your garden well, and as you entered adulthood, your philosophy became an obsession. You hungered for precious little things you could take and turn, worshipping their image as it manifested inside yourself. Your small religion made you reclusive and misunderstood, and you never had much luck in connecting to people. So it was only when you first saw them, feather-light and floating in their white dress; with skin like new lilies, that you realised that people were things too.

They were weak and you were insatiable. You spent the next few weeks memorising their routine, their mannerisms, the curves of their wrists. You practiced opening lines in front of a mirror until you were sure you sounded stupid, burying your face in a pillow in exasperation. Imagining kissing them with tongue, then taking their cane, or something bigger and heavier, and bashing their skull in so no one else would have a chance to hurt them. You would protect them from the horrors of monotony, misfortune, and malaise. How could you masturbate to something like that?

With great pleasure, you learnt the two of you shared a passion for stargazing. You were no stranger to the night's temptations, and often looked to the sky for answers in your sleepless seclusion. Now, with a curious intent, you stalked your shining star to their usual spot by the riverbank. With a heart beating like a moth's wings, you emerged from the shadows and stood beside them, staring at the city's reflection in the water. The night was too thick for them to see you blush at the sound of their breathing, and you shared that innocent moment together in silence until they pointed out a swan and her cygnets to you. You showed them the eagle constellation in response and they smiled.

Oh, it was torture. You saw the shine of the moon in their lip gloss, and the scent of lilacs growing near matched the colour of their eyes. They were so very beautiful.

You awkwardly dropped your gaze, then, so as not to see them turn from you. For a few minutes longer, you stood side by side - until they departed, their retreating silhouette a sliver of silver in the night. As soon as you were sure they would no longer look back, you shoved a fistful of lilacs into your mouth. The flowers had fed on the carbon dioxide they exhaled, and would purify your darkest thoughts. You needed to buy chloroform.

The preparations you made in the following weeks almost cost you your composure. When you ran into them at the local bookshop with a false sense of serendipity, the wry grin you wore as you imagined their shackled ankles almost gave you away. No, no - you wanted to cut their legs off and eat them as you watched them crawl around like a pup. They would be your helpless doll, a sacramental meal, and the only god in the world worshipped through desecration. You wanted to pluck out their eyes and sanctify your teeth with them, but you carried the conversation with all the dignity you still possessed. Did they flutter their lashes at you? You needed to prostrate yourself where you stood. Begging for forgiveness, you tore pages of poetry from their volumes and left the store with a mouthful of wet paper.

You did not meet a third time for fear of abusing the powers of coincidence. They missed you, no doubt. You, with an unusual depth to your words, a blush that reached your ears, and fingers that couldn't help twitching as you imagined wrapping them around their neck. How you pined for a casual coffee at their favourite cafe, an impromptu picnic at the park. Maybe they'd pick out an eagle pin to add to the strap of their bag as they loitered in the gift shop of the botanical gardens. You prayed they would not forget you.

The longer you waited for the perfect night, the deeper the sun set on your thoughts. The only light in your eyes was winged and predatory. Their celestial body would soon be yours to deflower, petals unravelling like a full moon becoming new again. The virgin crescent; the tears they'd cry; the light they shed on everything they touched would all be yours. You would kiss their fingertips and know chastity again, then sacrifice it all to kiss their shoulders and collarbones. They'd softly whimper when you'd slip your hands under their shirt and stroke their back, not daring to touch their breasts. They were almost flat-chested, almost - and it drove you crazy. On second thoughts, maybe you would feel them up after all, rubbing their nipples as you marked up their neck. They'd bruise wonderfully, with the yellowish tones of a wilted magnolia bud.

It was late spring, soon to be summer. Under a trinity of stars, you made nightly visits to the river. Your first few visits were fruitless, but it hardly discouraged you. Every constellation made up the freckles on their cheeks. The willow whispered to the ash, and all you could hear was their voice. Even the shapes of the flowing water reminded you of the pleats of their skirt being lifted by the wind. All your life, you had never known what being in love with another person felt like and dismissed it as a child's folly. Now, it devoured you.

When you saw them from your car on the fourth midnight, your heart felt like a dandelion shot through its ventricles. Chloroform rag in hand, you quietly walked over to them. Their ash-blond hair rippled in the breeze and gave a ghostly appearance to their slender figure. This was the single most important moment of your life.

This was the single most important moment of your life, and they turned around.

Without thinking, you tackled them to the ground, taking advantage of their bad leg. They shakily cried out in response, but were muffled by your hand. As you clamped the rag over their nose, their eyes flashed wide in fear. The full moon in bloom, the sky in surrender to you. They tried screaming again, but the knife in your other hand quickly convinced them that resistance was more dangerous than

129

compliance. Trying for reassurance, you shushed them and stroked their hair, but couldn't resist cutting a lock and bringing it to your lips. Severance was perfection, desecration was rebirth. You loved them more than anything, and stared into their filmy eyes as they slowly lost consciousness. It took three minutes but felt like the twenty-six years you were alive.

Finally, their body was limp underneath you. Gently, so gently, you closed their eyes shut and kissed each eyelid. You cradled them in your arms and carried them to your car, hoping more than anything that they recognised you. As you drove home, your hands trembled against the steering wheel. The words you muttered to yourself were nonsense: love was an act of consumption and consumption was an act of love. At last, at last, at last, at last, at last! The good things you consumed would make you good, and your hunger would be satiated at last.

ALTERNATIVE MEDICINE

I want to remodel the shape of your soul
With hands that repress and a knife that desires,
With scissors and scalpels and forceps and pliers:
Massaging your wounds and inverting you whole.

Your willingless flesh, the dim light in your eyes
Collapses the stars into scars on your skin.
What is life without sin? Wear a visceral grin
To our surgical altar of violent demise.

You're a sculpture of atrophy, misery's muse,
My manifest maid of malnourished elation,
A mouth made for morsels of manipulation!
So open it, darling - I'll put you to use.

I implore you, adore when you twist in refrain!
While shame may be sacred, I know you want more -
You hospital angel, you desperate whore,
You can't even tell between pleasure and pain!

It's torture! To be the sole witness of art,
To writhe as I watch with a feverish greed,
To want you! You've chiseled me into the need
To bleed like a body and beat like a heart!

You force me to doctor an intricate oath -
A passionate promise to bear like a ring.
I swear upon nothing but you, worthless thing:

When our hunger subsides I will murder us both.

THIS IS HOW I MADE THE WORLD

This is how I made the world.
Supernovae in a blender,
Edges effortlessly blurred,
Dust in intricate surrender.

Double helixed justice scales,
Lichen, nautilus, barbed wire,
Wind that swells in howling sails
As their captain dreams of fire.

Breaking waves, unbroken tides,
Serpents swallowing their tales
With a dear and dreadful pride,
Coiled, crowning thorns. Death-pale

Dawns, their lunar pawns advancing
With an outside inside curl,
Through the foliage it dances.
This is how I made the world.

Blades of grass, backs arched in wonder,
Fierce with rain's holy perversion.
Willing tongues to put it under,
Seashells sounding in recursion.

Desolation doubled over,
Forged through pleasure at the sun.
Mist and lightning, streaked and sober
With a song that's come undone.

Cold distortion, thrilled and livid -
Dissident in orphaned pearls.
Every color weird and vivid
As its cosmic chaos whirls.

Crucifixion and illusion,
Tortured orgasms deserved,
Sunsets smeared into confusion.
This is how I made the world.

Weeping wounds and whispered psalms,
Asphalt, steam, and benediction.
Halcyon and on and on
Blossoming into addiction,

Charm and friction and the heart,
Thick with salt and lust and grime.
Meat and benzene and pure art,
Twisting into honeyed rhyme.

And the end of time approaches,
Leeches tearing into skin,
Gossamer and out of focus,
Spider silk that yawns and spins.

Fractal lungs deluding devils
With the human tones of birds.
Watch the comets thrill and revel:
This is how I made the world.

Every forest ripe with games,
Midnight names and lucid reason
Drowned in a devoted flame,
Bending with the fleeting season.

Their delirium galvanic,
Elements combine and rise,
The grand motherboard organic
In her orchestrated eyes.

Curious and curious-
Lizard limbs and torn desire
Writhing loved and furious,
Circling a ceaseless pyre.

Glass that bubbles at the touch,
Walls that crumble at the word.
Everything and all too much.
This is how I made the world.

This is how I made the world:
Poetry that never yields,
Tears revealed, the needle stirred,
Rippled through a yellow field.

Mathematics, contemplation,
Sand, stigmata, source, the sea,
Tears, catharsis, adoration,
Angels lost on LSD.

Sounds of switchblades, neon silence,
Cyber veins wringed sevenfold.

Beautiful cascades of violence
Tapered into molten gold.

Force and power, strange and freeing,
Truth that favors the absurd,
All my love born into being:
This is how I made the world.

THE SURFACE OF A SERAPH

The devil's in the details, but God is in the axioms
And devotees of purity will rigorously bleed,
Enlightened by burst vessels, working abstracts to the
maximum:
Derivative of reverence, a lemma from the pieces.
In one of heaven's institutes, a succubus took seed:
A brilliant mathematician grew unhappy with their thesis.

An angel's work is tangible, not strung upon the ether -
And why create a seraph to deprive them of desire?
Discovery is hunger. In their analytic fever,
They grope for bodies like their own to classify for fun.
With lustful fingers feathering the figure of a fire,
The acolyte has chosen to triangulate the sun.

They lay her down on cosmic pitch and open her with praise:
How radiant you shine, my love - and soon, she will surrender
To a continuous scissor glide along her perfect rays.
Her corpse floats still and dull, no longer blinding but still
warm:
An oriented, bounded shell of former solar splendour.
Her body has unravelled and reduced to standard form.

Next is the moon: they'll take it like a Fibonacci starving
For sex and vivisection and a study of the shape -
Discarded with the knowledge that won't feed the vandal
carving
The sky to many shreds homeomorphic to each other.
They're all the same, and nothing leaves the angel's mouth
agape!

A true believer works until their theorem can smother

More brains with the obsession than they're keen to quantify.
There must be an alternative approach to seeking truth!
If mutilating those who rest upon beholders' eyes
Won't give a mathematician the desired happiness,
They will instead force meaning through a sieve of proper proof -
A page of inner beauty is required for success.

Who are they? A religious deviation from their study;
A vessel of Topology; a brave and playful thing!
So they will write and write until their talons come back bloody,
A poem of their own. A distillation of the verse.
A square and simple notebook tucked away under a wing
Holds everything they love, from the devout to the perverse.

Contracted to themself, their reason wavers in vibrato.
A madangel confined to their own body, their own mind,
Refines their chorus-voice to speak an ordinary motto:
I do believe in God. They bleed from geometric veins,
A shape so strange and right it cannot ever be defined
And oh, how it sustains me through the never-ending pain.

The seraph marks the paper with a fervent QED.
Aligning every edge, they fold the rectangle of words:
A torus genus one inscribed with all their poetry
Rests mortal in their hands, a newborn aspect of divinity.
The mathematician's faith, corrupt or pure, meets the absurd:
Their idol is a zero and a cycle of infinity.

OUR LADY OF THE REEDS

The river is an animal. It hunts, that beast, it feeds!
That feverish dominion of deep water and disaster
Will swallow up each daring man who deems himself her master,
And so we must pay tribute to our lady of the reeds.

She rises, sharp and radiant, and drops of human blood
Run red and stain her breasts with love we know not how to give,
Because she is divine, and she reminds us that we live
In reverence and fear of the forever promised flood.

At five years old, they tell me that I would not say a word.
I was to be surrendered, left to die in her embrace,
But she refused the summon, would not look upon my face.
She never takes the children, so my silence went unheard.

The years I learned to speak, they did not like what I would say.
I suffered, and grew dimmer, and survived by quiet song.
If being brave was wrong, I would just sigh and move along
Until the river's currents led my teenage heart astray.

I saw her first in winter, and my tears were quick to flow,
For she would die of thirst if I were destined to deny.
She drank them from my eyes and kissed my cheeks and said goodbye,
Evaporating fast into the glory of the snow.

I know she still remembers me, the girl who fed her verse
Under a swollen sky, my reason rhythmic in the rain.
In water, there is pain. I know that we will meet again,
The poets of our village disappearing by her curse.

Our sacrificial ferrymen destroy the thousandth tome,
But she is still so hungry, and my voice is what she needs.
My lady, stark and shivering, emerging from the reeds
To lay her wild claim upon the girl who leads her home.

THE PLANET VIEWED FROM SPACE, UNDER A MICROSCOPE

I'm wading in the shining sea whose urchins glow like stars.
My lungs are full of saltwater that stings against the scars
Inside of me, inside of me - I almost understand
How I don't need to burn to give the universe my light;
How sunbeams can be synthesised from shadows in the
night;
How I am right and true to hold the future in my hands.

I'm happy now. I've seen the summer wane and disappear,
But I am without fear, I swear - I hold the image dear:
I will outbloom the flowers, red and bright as I desire.
The birds perch on those wires that segment the vibrant sky,
And sing it from the heart before departing, born to fly.
The flutter of those wings sustains the memory of fire.

The sweetness of connection gives me strength to carry on,
Those station bells still ringing. Somewhere in Rostov-on-Don
A train has reached the platform, and I've reached the
shining shore.
Recovery, resentment, recognition, and reality -
New endings, old beginnings, and their effortless mortality
Awaiting me, returning me the universe and more.

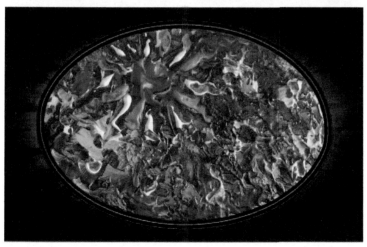

Printed in Great Britain
by Amazon

38485786R00086